THE
LITTLE BOOK OF
WORDS THAT
MATTER

MAGIC CAT 🐱 PUBLISHING

NEW YORK

CONTENTS

WELCOME TO

THE LITTLE BOOK OF
WORDS THAT MATTER

Finding the right word to describe something can feel comforting, exciting, and powerful.

In this book you'll find a collection of one hundred important words, carefully chosen in consultation with Wynne Kinder, M. Ed., a brilliant mindfulness educator. We selected words to help and inspire you to understand yourself and the world around you.

The book is split into four chapters:

FEELINGS MATTER
We explore emotions that everyone feels.

WE MATTER
We share how to be the best people we can be.

DIFFERENCES MATTER
We celebrate the beauty in each of us.

CHANGEMAKERS MATTER
We inspire you to make the world better.

On each page, you'll be invited to:

* Observe examples in your day-to-day life

* Practice positive affirmations (short, motivational statements)

* Move mindfully with breathing and yoga poses

* Ask questions and follow your curiosity

* Take care of yourself, your friends, and your family

Now we invite you to read on to grow—not only your vocabulary, but your hearts and minds, too.

ACCEPTED

When you feel **ACCEPTED**, you feel like
you belong just the way you are.

Being accepted can feel like . . .
A smile spreading across your face.
Wearing an outfit that feels great.
Others welcoming you with all the
things that make you special.

Feeling **ACCEPTED** is wonderful.
We can spread that wonderful feeling to others.
We can accept ourselves just as we are.
We can accept other people just as they are.

We can say hello!

We can invite others.

We can join in.

AFRAID

AFRAID is how you feel when you are scared or fearful. When you're afraid, you might hold your breath, cover your eyes, or hide to feel safe.

You might run away like a squirrel up a tree.

You might hide like a turtle.

You might whimper or growl like a dog.

Everyone feels **AFRAID** sometimes.

There are times when we need to be brave, too.
Being brave is taking action even when we're afraid.

You can practice being brave!

Stand tall like
a giraffe.

Put both hands
on your belly.

Breathe in through
your nose and feel
your belly fill.

Slowly let your breath
out. Say, "I am brave."

ANGRY

ANGRY is how you feel when you are mad.
It can feel like a thunderstorm in your body.

When we're angry, it can
be loud like thunder.

It can flash through us
quickly like lightning.

It can pour out of us like rain.

Thunderstorms don't last forever.
They pass with a little bit of time.
Feelings of anger pass with time, too.

Just like clouds moving through the sky, all emotions, including ANGER, come and go.

Start paying attention to the sky.

What does it look like in the morning?
Is it clear or cloudy?

What does it look like in the afternoon?
Is it the same or different?
What about in the evening?

ANXIOUS

ANXIOUS is how we feel when when we're worried
about something that could happen.

It can feel uncomfortable when we don't know
what to expect. We might not like
the feeling of not knowing.

Feeling anxious is tricky, because we can feel it
even if nothing frightening is happening at all!

Our bodies do different things when we feel **ANXIOUS**. Some people's fists scrunch up into balls. Some people feel flutters in their stomachs. Some people's hearts beat extra fast.

If that happens, try putting one hand on your heart and one hand on your belly. Breathe in through your nose and . . .

Send your breath to your fluttery belly . . .

Send your breath to your beating heart . . .

Send your breath to your open hands.

Say, "I am safe. I am loved. I can do my best."

APPRECIATIVE

Being **APPRECIATIVE** is a way of showing you are thankful.

When we are appreciative, we notice kind, caring, or special things people do. Then we take the time to show our thanks.

Being appreciative makes the people in our lives feel valued. We can make them feel good about themselves!

See if you can notice when others do kind, caring, or special things. Did someone make you a snack? Did a friend let you go first on the swing?

We're so lucky to have people who care about us. We can show we are APPRECIATIVE in simple ways. We can say . . .

"Thank you!"

"You're so thoughtful!"   "That was nice!"

When we are appreciative of others, we feel good, too.

ASHAMED

Feeling **ASHAMED** can come up when you feel like you've made a mistake or done something wrong. Sometimes the feeling comes when you are by yourself. Sometimes other people might lead you to feel ashamed.

You may get a big lump in your throat.

You may want to turn invisible.

You may feel frozen on the spot.

Feeling **ASHAMED** can be very tricky. It might make
you want to be quiet. It might make you want
to hide or stay away from others. But when
you feel ashamed, the best way to feel better
is to talk to someone who cares about you.

The important thing to remember is your friends
and family love you no matter what.

BORED

BORED is how you feel when you want to do something, but you can't think of anything interesting to do.

Being bored might sound like a grouchy "There's nothing to do!" or a long, loud s i g h . . .

Boredom can be a good thing! It means you're ready for lots of possibilities.

Try this the next time you're **BORED**.

1. Lie down and relax. You might think lying down is the opposite of interesting. But ideas have space to grow in your mind when you're calm and comfortable.

2. Use your body. Open your ears and listen for interesting sounds. Lift up your feet and let your feet look around! What do your feet see from their different point of view?

CONFUSED

CONFUSED is how you feel when you don't understand something. You might have too much information or not enough. Things might seem out of order. You might want to give up.

You can try simple things when you feel **CONFUSED.**

You can . . .

Pause

Slow down

Ask for help

Try again

CONTENT

When you are **CONTENT**, you feel peaceful. You're pleased with where you are, who you're with, and what you're doing.

Do you know how sometimes your body feels too hot or too cold? Other times, it feels just right. Feeling content is when your mind and body feel just right.

What helps you feel **CONTENT**? If you're not sure, pay attention the next time you feel that way.

What do your surroundings look like when you're calm and relaxed? What are you doing? What sounds and smells make you content?

When you notice these details, you'll know how to choose things that make you feel content, comfortable, and peaceful more often.

DETERMINED

When you feel **DETERMINED**, you feel confident and focused on a goal. A goal is something you want to learn, do, or make.

Being determined looks like . . . trying over and over again.

Being determined feels like . . . believing in yourself and what you can do.

Being determined sounds like . . . "I can do it."

Being DETERMINED starts with your thoughts.

☆ Think of something you want to learn, do, or make.

☆ Picture yourself reaching your goal. You can draw a picture or write it down.

☆ What is one thing you can do to reach your goal? When can you get started?

DISAPPOINTED

Being **DISAPPOINTED** can leave us feeling
like a deflated balloon.

We might feel
disappointed when
we were expecting
sun, but it rains.

Or when we can't go somewhere
we wanted to go.

We all feel **DISAPPOINTED** when things don't
go the way we want.

Naming how we feel is a good first step to moving
through it. We can say, "That's not what I wanted
to happen. I'm disappointed."

Then we can try to fill ourselves up again
by taking deep breaths in and out.
We can say . . .

"One good thing
is . . ."

"Next time,
we can . . ."

"What can we
do instead?"

EMBARRASSED

Feeling **EMBARRASSED** can be uncomfortable.

It can happen when someone sees us do
something we didn't want them to see.

When we're embarrassed . . .

Our cheeks may
feel hot.

Tears may fill our eyes.

We may feel like we want
to hide, or even shout.

Here's something to remember. When you say "I'm **EMBARRASSED**" to someone you trust, the feeling can get smaller, or it might even go away!

Some days, we are the ones who feel embarrassed. Other days, we see others who feel embarrassed. We might be able to help them feel better. We can say, "You're not the only one. That's happened to me, too!"

Sometimes our feelings can make us feel alone. It helps to know that all of us can have similar feelings.

EXCITED

EXCITED is how you feel when you are energetic and happy. When you're excited, your body wants to move. You might . . .

Squeal with delight

Clap your hands

Stretch your arms high

Jump up and down

Spin in a circle

There are lots of things to get **EXCITED** about . . .

Celebrating a holiday

Seeing something new

Discovering a surprise

When do you get excited? How does your body feel it? How does your body show it?

FRUSTRATED

When we're really trying but still having a hard time, we might feel **FRUSTRATED**.

Feeling frustrated is tough. It can lead to other strong feelings, like anger or sadness.

When we're frustrated, we might blame something or someone else. We might want to give up. We might say, "I can't do it!"

Everybody feels **FRUSTRATED** at times.

The good thing is, we can try different
ways to work through it. We can...

Take a break

Breathe deeply
to feel calm

Ask for help

Try again

What could you say or do if you saw a friend
feeling frustrated?

GRATEFUL

GRATEFUL is how we feel when we appreciate or are thankful for what is good in our lives.

We can find things to be grateful for by using our senses.
Our eyes can look for something beautiful.
Our ears can listen for friendly voices.
Our noses can smell fresh, clean air.
Our hands can hug people we love.

Try playing a **GRATEFUL** game with a friend or family member. Take turns asking questions.

What is something you're grateful your body can do?

What is something you are grateful for in your home?

Who is someone you are grateful for in your community?

What is something you are grateful for on our planet?

You can play this game over and over again. The more you look for good things, the more good things you see.

JEALOUS

When you want something that someone else
has, you might feel JEALOUS.

Feeling jealous can come with other feelings,
like frustration, anger, or sadness.

You could feel jealous from wanting . . .
A toy. A turn.
Some time. Some attention.

When you feel JEALOUS, you can practice . . .

Solving a problem

Can we please share?

May I please have a turn?

Would you like to swap?

Paying attention to what you have

Patience

It might be hard, but you can do it.

JOYFUL

JOYFUL is how you feel when you spot, make, give, or spread happiness.

Feeling joyful can lead you to skip, jump, or bounce.
You can feel curious and quiet.
You can feel delighted, pleased, and proud.

Think about the moments, activities, or things that make you feel **JOYFUL**.

What is something that makes you joyful in each season of the year?

Picking flowers in Spring?

Keeping cool in Summer?

Crunching dry, colorful leaves in autumn?

Wearing soft, furry hats and socks in winter?

Keep growing your collection of joyful moments every day.

LONELY

LONELY is how we feel when we want
to talk or play with someone, but we can't.

We might feel lonely if
we feel different.

We might feel lonely if
we're left out of a game.

We might feel lonely
if someone is busy.

The funny thing about feeling lonely is that
lots of people feel the same way!

When you feel **LONELY**, you can . . .

Tell someone how you feel

Look for friends, real or imaginary

Ask for what might make you feel better

After a bit of time, a friend or family member might be ready to talk or play!

LOVED

When you feel **LOVED**, you feel safe, cared for, and appreciated.

People know they are loved when they see . . .

Warm Smiles

Open arms

Wagging tails

How does your family show you they love you?
How could you show your family you love them?

You can make yourself feel **LOVED**, too!

When you love and care for yourself, you can love all things even more.

Make a bracelet for yourself or someone you love.

You can use beads, thread, wool, or even recycled items.

Give your bracelet to someone with the message:
"You are loved."

NERVOUS

When you are **NERVOUS**, you might
have a jittery, fidgety feeling.

You might feel uneasy about doing
something. Sometimes nervousness is
excitement in disguise.

Your face
may sweat.

Umm . . .

Your voice
may wobble.

Your stomach
may hurt.

Your knees
may shake.

Everyone feels nervous once in a while,
even grown-ups.

The next time you feel **NERVOUS**, try thinking about something silly.

Try making a silly sound, a silly face, or a silly shape with your body.

Maybe you'll laugh! Laughing is a good way to get nervous or excited energy out of our body. Plus, laughing is so much fun.

OFFENDED

You might feel **OFFENDED** if someone says or does something that hurts your feelings.

It's OK to let them know. You can say . . .

"I don't like how you're playing."

"That wasn't nice."

"That hurts my feelings."

You can give them a chance to do better next time.

Sometimes a friend might be **OFFENDED** by
something you say or do.

Everyone makes mistakes with their friends.
When a problem comes up and you notice
someone is offended, you can . . .

Take a break.
Come back and talk about it.
Work it out.

When you offend someone, you can learn how to
do better or show more care the next time.

OVERWHELMED

OVERWHELMED is how you feel when everything is **TOO MUCH**.

It might feel like there are too many things to look at, too many sounds, too many thoughts in our heads.

Even lots of good things can make us feel confused and stressed.

Calming your body helps your brain when you feel **OVERWHELMED**. Practice calming your body when you're able to find a quiet space.

Put your palms together.

Hold your hands in front of your heart.

Take one breath in. Let one breath out.

Take another breath in. Let that breath out.
Say, "I can do one thing at a time."

PROUD

To feel **PROUD** is to feel good about yourself.

It looks like a grin and bright eyes.

It sounds like, "I did it! I'm proud of myself!"

It feels like standing tall with a full heart.

Write down, draw pictures, or take photographs
of moments that make you feel PROUD.

It's fun to look back at what we're proud of
and share our happiness with others.

When we remember what we've achieved, we believe
in ourselves. When we believe in ourselves, we
can set our minds to achieve anything.

SAD

When you are SAD, you feel unhappy.

Like all feelings, sometimes you feel a little
bit. Sometimes you feel a lot.

At times, sadness might feel heavy, dark, or gloomy.

Sadness might feel empty, like a toy box that
was full and now has nothing inside.

It can take a time for sadness to pass.

Treat yourself gently when you're feeling **SAD.**

Think about things that are soothing to you and find, or even make, a peaceful place.

Create a space where you can draw, read, listen to music, talk to someone you love, cuddle, or rest.

Discover what is soothing to you so you can return to it whenever you need comfort.

SHY

SHY is how you feel when you are nervous or not ready to meet or talk to other people. You might feel especially shy around people you don't know yet.

There are lots of things you can do if
you're feeling SHY.

You can take
small steps.

It's OK to take
your time.

You can get closer
when you're ready.

You can make
a new friend.

A new friend
can meet you.

What can you do when others feel shy? How might
you make someone feel comfortable and welcome?

ACCOMPLISH

You ACCOMPLISH a goal when you set out to do
something and you complete it.

It takes a few steps to accomplish a goal.

Say, "I can!"

Say, "I will!"

Say, "I did!"

You can celebrate yourself when you
ACCOMPLISH something big or small.

Name what you
accomplished.

I made
an origami
banner!

Well
done!

Remember all the things you
did to reach your goal.

Share your accomplishments with family and friends.
Let them celebrate you, too!

APOLOGIZE

Sometimes we feel bad for something we did wrong, or if something happens by accident.

When we **APOLOGIZE**, we say and show that we are sorry.

I'm sorry.

We can **APOLOGIZE** to show the other person that we care about them and their feelings.

When we make mistakes, we might feel all kinds of strong feelings.

The other person might have strong feelings, too.

An apology can help the other person feel better and it can make us feel better, too.

This is even better than before!

Have you ever apologized to a friend?
How did you feel afterward?

AUTHENTIC

AUTHENTIC means real. You're being authentic when you say or do things that make you feel like you. You aren't pretending to be like someone else.

Sometimes you like the same things as your friends. Sometimes you don't.

Sometimes you'll change your mind. Sometimes you won't.

Being **AUTHENTIC** feels good. It feels comfortable sharing what you like and dislike, what you're good at and what you're still learning, and even who you are when you're doing nothing at all.

Write a name poem and celebrate things about yourself.

Write down the letters of your name, one on each line, going down.

Artist
Nice
Noisy
Excitable

Using each letter, think of a word or phrase that describes you.

Feel good about being the authentic and true you!

CAPABLE

When we are **CAPABLE**, we are able to do something.

We've watched, learned, and practiced.

We have the skills we need.

Have you ever been surprised by what you could do?

You're CAPABLE of so much!

What are you capable
of doing to take care
of your clothes?

What are you capable
of doing to take care
of your home?

What are you capable
of doing to take care
of your pets?

What are you capable
of learning how to do?

CHOICE

A **CHOICE** is when you get to pick or choose.

Our choices have power.

We can make choices that . . .

Help us grow
healthy and strong

Show our friends
we care

Keep our neighborhoods clean

What CHOICES can you make to protect our planet?

Turn off the lights

Eat more plants

Recycle at home

Turn off the water

Walk to school

Our choices can make a difference!

CONFIDENT

When you're **CONFIDENT**, you feel good
about yourself and what you can do.

Confidence can come from . . .

Practicing over
and over

Believing in
yourself

Trying again
after failing

Learning more

Practice feeling **CONFIDENT** with this star pose.
See what it is like to take up space and feel big.

Stretch your arms
out to your sides.

Step your feet
wide apart.

Lift up the corners
of your mouth.

Say, "I am confident!"

Does your body feel stronger?

CONSENT

Your body is YOUR body. Every part—
from your hair to your belly button to your toes.

Your friend's body is THEIR body. Every part—
from their hair to their belly button to their toes.

You decide what actions are OK for you
and your body, and your friends decide what
actions are OK for them and their bodies.

Asking for CONSENT is a way to ask others
what actions are OK for their bodies.

Ask for **CONSENT** when you want to do things like touch, hug, or tickle someone.

They give consent when they say yes.

If they say or show no, that means stop.

If they don't say anything, that means stop, too.

We all get to decide what we want for our own bodies!

CREATIVE

Being **CREATIVE** is using your imagination.

Being creative is . . .

Playing an instrument

Making up a song

Choosing clothes

Drawing a picture

And so much more!

Being **CREATIVE** can be anything.

Being creative can be everything!

Play around and get creative. Look around
for things that inspire you.

Find treasure

Arrange treasure

Make treasure

CURIOUS

When we're **CURIOUS**, we ask a lot of questions.
We wonder. We imagine. We think about possibilities.

"Where does that come from?"

"What would happen if . . . ?"

"Why does that happen?"

"How can I learn more?"

Do you have any plants in or around your home?

Take a closer look at them.

Investigate the soil, stem, and leaves.

What colors
do you see?

What do they
smell like?

What do they
feel like?

Check out the plants next week. Do you think
they will look different or the same?

What else are you CURIOUS about?

ENCOURAGE

People can **ENCOURAGE** us. They can have confidence in us and share it with us!
They can . . .

Give us a boost

Hold us steady

Believe in us

Give us a push

Watch us go

Cheer for us

We can **ENCOURAGE** others, too.
We can . . .

Hold their
hands

Pick them up

I know you
can do it!

Go step-by-step

Give a hug

Cheer for
them

Watch
them go

How do you feel when someone encourages you?
How do you feel when you encourage someone else?

FAILURE

FAILURE is when we try something but we don't succeed. It might not feel good to fail, but it's an important part of reaching a goal.

As we learn how to walk, we trip.

As we learn how to tie, we get tangled.

As we learn how to scoot, we stumble.

FAILURE can feel like a strong word. But it just means we're trying and learning.

We try. We fail. We learn a little. We try again. And sometimes again and again and again!

Try balancing on one leg. Whoa!

Did you fall over?

Keep trying.

Over time, see if you're able to stand on one leg longer and longer.

Falling and failing helps you figure out how to finally succeed.

FRIENDSHIP

FRIENDSHIP is a connection between two people. A friend is someone you know and like and who knows and likes you.

Friendship can feel relaxing.

It can feel energizing.

It can sound quiet.

It can sound loud.

It can be filled with liking the same things—or different things!

The next time you're with a friend, take a picture.

Keep a copy for yourself and send one to your friend.

You'll both have a special memento of your **FRIENDSHIP.**

What do you like to do with your friends?

HEALTHY

We feel **HEALTHY** when our bodies and brains are working well and we feel good.

There are so many ways to keep ourselves healthy and safe. We can . . .

Move our bodies

Eat fruits and vegetables

Wear a helmet

Protect our skin from the sun

Spending time outdoors is another way
to stay **HEALTHY.**

What is something you like to do outdoors
that makes you feel healthy?

Invite a friend or family member to join you.

Enjoying time with others is another way
to keep our minds and bodies healthy!

INDEPENDENT

We are **INDEPENDENT** when we can do something on our own.

It might sound like . . .

"I don't need help!"

"I know how!"

"I can do it myself!"

It might look like a proud smile.

You can be **INDEPENDENT** in lots of ways.

Do you have a library card? If not, see if you can sign up for one at your local library.

You can be independent and choose your very own books.

With a library card, books, and your imagination, you can go anywhere and do anything.

MINDFUL

When we're **MINDFUL**, we pay attention to our bodies in the present moment—the right now. We focus on what we feel in our bodies.

Do you ever feel relaxed and refreshed after a nice, warm bath?

Practicing mindfulness can give your brain and body a relaxed and refreshed feeling.

Explore your five senses with this **MINDFUL** activity.

Sit or lie down.

Close your eyes and take a deep breath in.

Open your eyes—
what colors do
you see?

Open your nose—
what do you smell?

Open your ears—
what sounds do
you hear?

Open your hands—
what do you feel?

Open your mouth—
what do you taste?

Take your time and discover how much you notice.

MISTAKE

Whoops! A **MISTAKE** is when we make a choice that turns out wrong.

There are lots of words to describe mistakes.

That's because there are lots of ways to make mistakes.

Drop

Miss

Slip-up

Mix-up

Spill

Lose

There are lots of ways to learn from mistakes, too.

The next time you make a **MISTAKE**, try saying, "Whoops!"

Then think about how you might be able to do something different in the future.

You can say, "I learned from last time . . ." "Next time I will . . ."

PRACTICE

If we want to learn how to do something really well, we can **PRACTICE!**

Practicing is a way of training our brains and bodies to do something new, like . . .

Performing a
magic trick

Playing the drums

Scoring a goal

Doing a cartwheel

PRACTICE doing something new—and a little silly!

See how long you can balance a book or a stuffed animal on your head.

Once you get the hang of it, try taking a walk.

How far can you get before dropping it?

What would you like to learn how to do?
How could you practice?

RESILIENCE

Have you played in shallow water at the beach?

Sometimes a wave can knock you over, but after it passes, you can get back up.

Lots of things in life can make us feel knocked over.

You might face challenges that make you feel sad, angry, or frustrated.

Showing **RESILIENCE** is when you're able to get back up and keep going.

There are lots of things you can do to build your own RESILIENCE.

Talk to someone about how you feel.

Think of ways to solve a problem.

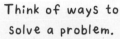

Look for the positives.

Find things that help you feel calm.

Learn from your mistakes.

Keep trying!

RESOURCEFUL

Being RESOURCEFUL means using what we already
have in a creative way.

We can find solutions to problems when
we're resourceful.

Being resourceful helps us save money.

It can help us save the planet, too!

Before buying something new, try being
RESOURCEFUL at home.

You can be resourceful when you give gifts.

You can be resourceful when you wrap gifts, too.

Spark your creativity by using newspaper,
magazines, or even your collection of drawings.

Being resourceful is a way to feel proud.

RESPONSIBLE

When you're **RESPONSIBLE**, you're someone who can be counted on to make good choices.

Being responsible means doing what you say you will.

How can you show that you are responsible in your home?

Water your plants

Make your bed

Care for your toys

Feed your pets

We can be **RESPONSIBLE** inside and outside our homes—in our neighborhood and beyond.

When everyone does their part to be responsible, we share a cleaner, healthier, safer world.

How can each of us be responsible in our community?

SELF-AWARE

"Aware" is just another way of saying that we're paying attention. We're **SELF-AWARE** when we pay attention to what we think, say, and do.

When we pay attention, we understand ourselves better. We can notice what makes us feel accepted, comfortable, and happy.

Being self-aware also means being able to recognize how other people see us.

Our actions can help others feel accepted, comfortable, and happy, too.

Explore your face and become more **SELF-AWARE**.

Stand in front of a mirror.

Lift the corners of your mouth way up high. Open your eyes wide.

Raise your eyebrows. Can you raise one at a time?

Lower your eyebrows and squeeze them together.

Now make as many funny faces as you can!

How do you look now?

Did you notice anything new about your face?

Play around with feeling faces. How could you use your face to show that you're happy to see someone, or that you're sorry when they are unhappy?

STRENGTH

We all have different **STRENGTHS**. These are things we are good at or do well.

Our strengths change over time.

What are some of your strengths?

Drawing

Catching a ball

Making up stories

Being a good friend

You get better and better at things by practicing.

You can practice noticing the **STRENGTHS** in others.

When you see someone doing a good job,
let them know.

One of your strengths can be uplifting and
celebrating the people around you!

SUPPORT

SUPPORT is another word for "help."

We can support others who are having a hard time.

Everyone needs support sometimes.

People who are sick

People who are sad

People who are lonely

People who are scared

Think of ways you can **SUPPORT** others.
What could you say?

I hope you get well soon!

Can I help?

I'm listening.

You may need support sometimes, too.
What could you say?

Can I tell you something?

I don't feel very well.

Can you help me?

TRUST

TRUST is believing someone cares about you
and will do their best for you.

You can tell the truth to someone you trust and
they tell the truth to you, too.

Someone you trust makes you feel safe.

TRUST comes from . . .

Telling the truth

Doing what you
Say you'll do

I'll catch you!

Admitting when you've
made a mistake

Being there when
someone needs you

It's really special when people trust you.

WORTHY

You have something in common with every person in the whole world: You are **WORTHY**!

Being worthy means that you're important and that you matter.

We don't have to do anything special or be anything special. We are worthy just as we are.

Every person in every place is **WORTHY**.

We are worthy of . . .

Love and
friendship

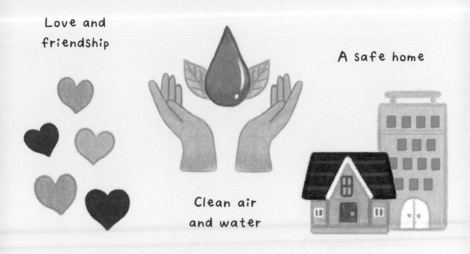

Clean air
and water

A safe home

Try this simple exercise to help you feel worthy.

Sit in a
comfortable
position.

Put both hands
over your heart.

Say to yourself,
"I am worthy."

ABILITY

An **ABILITY** is something you are able to do.

Peacocks have the ability to walk. Hummingbirds have the ability to fly. Penguins have the ability to swim. Ducks can do all three—walk, fly, and swim!

Like birds, humans have the **ABILITY** to do lots of different things.

Some things are easy to learn, and some are harder.

Some things come quickly for one person, but may take more time for someone else.

Having different abilities comes in handy. We can teach one another. And we can use our different abilities to accomplish big things.

BODY

Your **BODY** is amazing! It includes your bones, your muscles, and your organs—like your brain, heart, lungs, stomach, and skin.

All of your body parts work together to keep you alive, healthy, and capable.

How do you take care of your body?

Take a moment to appreciate your **BODY**
and all that it does for you!

To my brain, thank you
for learning new things.

To my lungs, thank
you for each breath.

To my heart, thank
you for every beat.

To my stomach,
thank you for turning
food into energy.

To my skin, thank you
for protecting me
from head to toe.

Now shake, swing, stretch, or move in any way
that feels good to your body!

BELONGING

We feel a sense of **BELONGING** when we are welcomed and accepted.

We can feel a sense of belonging in our families, our classrooms, and in our communities.

We can even feel a sense of belonging when we read books and see characters who look, think, or act like we do.

How do you feel when you meet someone new?
Shy? Excited? Curious?

Playing a game is a fun way to get to know
someone new and to let them get to know you.

When you invite a friend to join, play, imagine,
or build with you, you create a feeling of
BELONGING for you both!

What games do you like to play? What game
would be good to play with a group?

COMMUNITY

A **COMMUNITY** is a group that has something in common.

Our school is a community of people who learn together.

Our hobbies can give us a community of people who like the same things.

Our neighborhood is a community of people who live in the same place.

Our community can include people who share the same beliefs and different ones, too.

What is one **COMMUNITY** you belong to?

Draw a picture of it.
You could draw . . .

The people in
your community

What you do with
your community

The place where your
community gathers

What does your community share or have in common?

CONNECTION

A **CONNECTION** is made when two or more things or people join together.

In life, friends connect with each other in many ways.

Liking the
same foods

Adoring the
same animals

Listening to the
same music

What's a **CONNECTION** you have with friends?

Doing a jigsaw puzzle with a friend is a great way to connect.

As you work together to join the pieces one by one, you can create something beautiful.

CULTURE

CULTURE is a word that describes a group of people's ways of life, or how they do things.

Culture can include language, food, clothing, music, and art. Your culture can come from where you live and where your family is from.

Cultures can mix and change over time. There are almost two hundred countries in the world, and each country has its own culture . . . and many have more than one!

Ahurea

Cultura תַרְבּוּת

فرهنگ Kulttuuri

문화 Culture 文化

Πολιτισμός Kultur

Budaya संस्कृति культура

Cultuur văn hóa

วัฒนธรรม

You might think that everyone acts the same way when they meet for the first time. But people greet each other differently depending on their CULTURE.

Some wave, shake, or clap their hands.

Some bow their heads. Others press their foreheads.

Some kiss on the cheek once, twice, or even three times.

How do people greet one another in your culture?

DISABILITY

A **DISABILITY** is when part of your body or brain works differently from most people. It can make it difficult to see, hear, speak, move around, learn, think, or make friends.

Some disabilities can be seen by others.

Some disabilities can't.

Some disabilitites last for a short time.

Some disabilities last a longer time.

Many people have some kind of **DISABILITY.**

Do you have a disability?

Do you know anyone who has a disability?

How are you like your friends?

How are you different?

DISAGREE

To **DISAGREE** means to think differently from someone else about a topic.

Family members love one another.
Friends have fun together.
Family members can disagree with one another and friends can disagree, too.

You might disagree about little things.

You might disagree about big things.

Our family needs a dog.

We can't get a dog.

When people disagree, they might argue or get upset.

It's OK to **DISAGREE.**

Sometimes it's fun to try to get another person to agree with us.

Other times, we might be the ones to change our minds.

Lots of times, we accept our differences and move along!

DIVERSITY

DIVERSITY means differences.

Our world has a lot of diversity.

We have people of different ages.

We have people from different cultures.

Our own communities have a lot of diversity, too.

We have people with different families.

We have people with different religions.

When a diverse group of people share ideas, works together, and solves problems, we can create beauty, peace, and joy.

Create your own joyful garden of DIVERSITY.

Scatter different kinds of seeds.

Water the soil.

Watch your beautiful garden bloom.

EQUITY

We all want to be safe and healthy. We all want to have fair choices and to have fun.

EQUITY is about making sure things are fair and that everyone has access to what they need.

It's important to notice when things are fair and when they're not.

When we see problems with equity, then we can think about how to solve them.

We can work to make things safe, healthy, fair, and fun for all.

There are lots of opportunities to achieve **EQUITY** for everyone.

Look around the places where you spend time.

Can everyone access them?

Can everyone move around freely?

Is everyone able to be safe and happy?

How could these places be fairer and provide everyone what they need?

ETHNICITY

ETHNICITY is a way to describe yourself.

Some people think about their ethnicity as related to the place where their ancestors (family from a long, long, long time ago) were from. Others think about their religion as their ethnicity. Ethnicity can also include the language you speak or your cultural traditions.

You can discover a lot about yourself and your
ETHNICITY by talking to your family.

Your ethnicity can give you . . .

Events and
traditions

Stories and
celebrations

Shared languages

A strong community   A sense of belonging

FAMILY

A FAMILY is a group of people who love and care about one another.

Every family is special and unique.
Some families are big.
Some families are small.
Some families are spread out all over the world.
Some families all live in the same place.

There are all kinds of combinations of families.
There are all kinds of love and care.

Celebrate your **FAMILY** by making each member an award.

Your awards can be thoughtful, fun, or silly!

While every family is different, all families are special.

GENDER

When we talk about ourselves, we often include our GENDER.

Some people describe their gender as a man or boy. Some people describe their gender as a woman or girl.

You might feel strongly about the one that feels right to you. You might feel like you are a little bit of both, or like neither.

You're the best person to know what matches how you feel.

People can express **GENDER** in different ways.
Express means to match the way you look on the
outside with the way you feel on the inside.

What kinds of clothes make you feel comfortable
right now?

How do you like wearing your hair?

What do you like to call yourself?

IDENTITY

Our **IDENTITY** is made up of the many details that make each of us who we are.

Identity can include where we live, where our family is from, what we enjoy, or even what sports teams we like.

Sometimes people assume, or guess, about parts of our identity by what we look like on the outside. But often the best way to learn about people is to talk with them and listen.

Explore all the different parts of your IDENTITY by making a "tree of me."

Draw a tree with lots of branches.

On each branch, write a word that describes you.

It's beautiful to see the many parts of who we are.

INCLUSIVE

Being **INCLUSIVE** means including everyone.

Sometimes people are left out because of their gender, religion, race, or disability. To be inclusive is to make sure everyone can join in.

When we're included, we might feel comfortable, happy, accepted, or proud.

When we're excluded and left out, we might feel lonely, sad, frustrated, or angry.

I'd like to play, too.

We can be INCLUSIVE by . . .

Noticing others

Play with us!

Reaching out

Listening

Inviting others

When we're inclusive, we open up to the possibilities of friendship, creativity, and fun.

LISTEN

To LISTEN means to give our attention to what someone is saying. Listening is a way of showing others that we care.

When we listen . . .

We are inspired

We connect

We grow

We learn

Did you know that you can use your whole body to **LISTEN**?

You use your ears to hear people's voices.

You nod your head to show you understand.

You focus and look in others' eyes.

You turn your chest and heart toward others to show you're open to hearing what they have to say.

The next time you're in a conversation, try using your whole body to listen. See if you feel a difference or if you see a difference in the person you're with.

LEARN

We **LEARN** every day in all kinds of ways.

We learn by . . .

Watching and listening

Trying and failing

Exploring and discovering

Practicing and performing

It's great when we **LEARN** something new.

Learning makes so many things possible.

What would you like to learn more about?

Think about a friend or someone in your family.

What would you like to learn from them?

What might they want to learn from you?

NEURODIVERGENT

Each of us is a little different.

We think, learn, and experience the world in our own ways.

Some of us are **NEURODIVERGENT**. Neuro means related to the brain. Divergent means different. This means our brains work in different ways.

When you're **NEURODIVERGENT**, you might prefer doing things in the same order every day, having a quiet and peaceful space, or being able to move around.

How do you feel when your space is quiet? What do you notice when your space is a little noisy? When do you like to move around?

All of us are the same in important ways: We are all capable and worthy of learning, having fun, and feeling accepted.

PROGRESS

PROGRESS means getting better over time.

Progress usually doesn't happen all at once.

It can feel exciting.

It can also feel frustrating.

Sometimes it's hard to tell if we're making any **PROGRESS**.

Progress comes from trying and failing, and trying and failing again.

But with time and patience, it can also feel like we're flying high.

RACE

RACE is a term used to group people together based on the way they look. For years, the word race has been used to describe the color of people's skin.

In fact, skin color is based on something called melanin. Melanin is inside our bodies. Each person has a different amount. The more melanin we have in our bodies, the darker our skin appears. Melanin also affects our hair and eye color.

When people talk about **RACE**, you may hear about black, white, and brown. When you look around, there are countless wonderful skin, hair, and eye colors.

How would you describe your skin, hair, and eye color?

How do you and your family members look similar? In what ways are you different?

Isn't it interesting to see how we're alike and different?

RELIGION

A **RELIGION** is a group of beliefs about the world.

Many religions practice a way of praying that includes giving thanks for the good things in life.

How do you practice giving thanks for the good things in your life?

Lots of **RELIGIONS** have special buildings where people gather together.

Buddhism has viharas.

Christianity has churches.

Hinduism has mandirs.

Islam has mosques.

Judaism has synagogues.

Sikhism has gurdwaras.

Where do you go to practice your religion if you have one?

REPRESENTATION

REPRESENTATION is the way that people are shown or described. We can see representations of people in books, TV shows, movies, and toys.

When we see people like us represented, we might feel excited.

When we see people like us represented in the same ways over and over again, we might feel disappointed.

And when we don't see ourselves at all, we might feel invisible.

REPRESENTATION is important.

Start to look around with some extra attention.

What kinds of dolls do you see?

Who do you see in books? What are they doing?

On TV, what kinds of families do you see?

Do you notice any kinds of people missing?

It's wonderful when all kinds of people are represented in ways that feel right and true.

RESPECT

RESPECT is a way to show care and kindness.

We show respect by listening and by paying attention to another person's thoughts and feelings.

We can remind others to show us **RESPECT**, too.

It's normal to argue or disagree with someone.

Maybe they'll change their mind and see our point of view.

Maybe they won't.

We can still respect one another . . .
and have fun together.

TRADITION

A **TRADITION** is a special activity that is repeated, sometimes year after year.

Eating and decorating with watermelons is a popular tradition to welcome the Vietnamese Lunar New Year, known as Tet Holiday. People believe that red is a lucky color. Watermelons are red and sweet, so they are thought to bring luck and sweetness into people's lives.

Many religions have **TRADITIONS** that include foods.

It's traditional to dip apples in honey for Rosh Hashanah, the Jewish New Year.

During the Hindu festival of Diwali, people eat motichoor ladoo, round balls made with sugar, spices, and nuts.

Hot cross buns are traditionally eaten during the Christian feast of Easter.

What are some of your family's food traditions? Do you know why you eat those foods? Finding out about your own traditions and the traditions of others is a fun way to explore different cultures.

UNIQUE

Each one of us is UNIQUE!

Unique means unlike anything or anybody else.
Something is unique when it's the only one of its kind.

No one else in the whole world is exactly like you.

You have a unique and special voice.
You have a unique and special laugh.
You have a unique and special smile.
You even have a unique and special tongue!

Explore how **UNIQUE** you are by looking in a mirror.

Stick out your tongue!

Every person's tongue has its own shape and texture. The way the tiny bumps and ridges are spread out on your tongue is unique to you.

Now look at your ear. Trace the rim of your ear with your finger. Can you feel the curves and ridges? You're the only person with those exact ones.

You are so unique and special.
Every human you know is, too . . .
we all have that in common!

ACTIVISM

ACTIVISM is when you take action to make the changes you want to see in the world.

Step 1: Notice a problem.

Step 2: Think of ways to solve the problem or make it smaller.

Step 3: Take action.

ACTIVISM makes a difference!

It might take a lot of people.

It might take a lot of tries.

It might even take a lot of time.

Plant a Tree for the Earth Today!

But it can start with one person, taking one idea, one step at a time.

ALLY

An **ALLY** is a person who steps in when someone is being treated badly.

Sometimes, we need an ally to support us. It hurts to be treated unfairly, and having an ally can help us feel understood and safe.

Other times, we can be an ally to someone else.

To be an **ALLY**, we can...

Speak up

What you
said was
mean.

Listen

We can show kindness to others and stand
up for what is fair and right.

ANTI-RACISM

ANTI-RACISM has two parts.

The first part is understanding racism. That's when people are treated unfairly because of their race. Some are treated better, and some are treated worse.

The second part of anti-racism is knowing that racism is wrong and working toward stopping it.

We can practise **ANTI-RACISM** by paying attention
to any unfairness around us.

Sometimes we judge others based on their race
without even knowing we're doing it.

Sometimes we are judged by others because
of our race.

We can work together to make things better.
We can listen. We can learn.

BOUNDARY

You have a **BOUNDARY** around your body.
It's like an invisible bubble around you.

You can put your boundary up when you feel like
someone is too close and you want more space.

You can put your boundary down when you
want to be close, or receive a hug.

You're in charge of your boundary.

Telling others about your boundaries isn't always easy. It gets easier the more you practice.

Here are some things you can say when you want to set a **BOUNDARY**.

"I feel uncomfortable. Stop."

"I need space."

"You're playing too rough."

Everyone has boundaries for their own bodies. Pay attention and respect their boundaries too.

CELEBRATE

When we **CELEBRATE**, we take time to enjoy happy events.

We get together to show we care.

It can look like . . .

It can taste like . . .

It can sound like . . .

We can **CELEBRATE** the achievements that lead to greater peace, freedom, and happiness in our communities.

We can celebrate all kinds of love.

We can celebrate firsts.

We can celebrate progress.

What special days and occasions do you celebrate?

COMMUNICATE

To **COMMUNICATE** is to express information, thoughts, and feelings.

We communicate with our faces.

We communicate with our bodies.

We communicate by speaking and listening.

We communicate by reading and writing.

Here's a surprise: A big part of communicating is actually being quiet.

We can **COMMUNICATE** that we care when we give people our attention. This could mean . . .

stopping what
we're doing,

facing them,

looking them
in the eye

and listening.

COMPROMISE

A **COMPROMISE** is a solution when people want different things.

In a compromise, each person gives up a little of what they want and gets a little of what they want.

People work together so that both sides are content.

You can take turns.

You can share.

You can work it out.

A **COMPROMISE** shows that we have respect
and understanding for others.

CONSERVATION

CONSERVATION is using Earth's resources
in careful ways so they're not wasted.

Water is one of Earth's most valuable resources.
We wash in it, clean with it, drink it, and use it to
produce everything from clothing to food. Animals
and plants need it, too!

We can do small things every day to conserve
water. Everything we do adds up.

CONSERVATION is an important way you can help the planet.

Conserve water by turning off the faucet when you brush your teeth.

Only pour the amount of water you can drink. If you have extra, share it with your houseplants instead of pouring it down the drain.

Collect and reuse rainwater. What else could you do with rainwater around your home?

COURAGE

COURAGE is a feeling that comes from inside us.

Courage helps us do things that are difficult.

It helps us do things that make us nervous, anxious, or scared.

Lots of times, feeling nervous comes first.
That's OK! Courage can follow.

It might take time and practice to feel
your **COURAGE** build up.

You can try . . .

Saying how
you feel

Telling yourself,
"I can do this."

Taking a few
slow, full
breaths

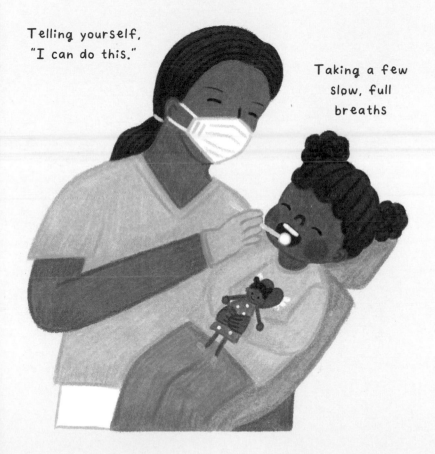

Your courage can rise up inside you,
one breath at a time.

EMPATHY

Our bodies can get hurt sometimes.
We may trip, fall, and bruise our body.

Our feelings get hurt sometimes, too.
We may trip, fall, and feel embarrassed.

EMPATHY is understanding how someone
feels because you can imagine what it's like
to be them. You can imagine yourself in their
place and feel what they might be feeling.

Having **EMPATHY** helps you to be a good friend.

You can get better and better at having empathy.

You can give your attention to a friend's facial expressions and body language.

You can imagine yourself in their shoes.

You can ask questions.

You can listen.

EMPOWER

When you **EMPOWER** someone, you make them feel powerful. You help them feel capable and confident.

You can empower someone by . . .

Teaching them a new skill.
Cheering them on.
Celebrating their success.

You can also **EMPOWER** yourself. You can make yourself feel powerful. You can feel capable and confident by learning new skills, cheering yourself on, or celebrating your successes.

When you want to empower yourself, try saying:
"My brain is powerful.
My body is powerful.
I am powerful."

How could you move your body or stretch your brain as you say these things to feel even stronger?

FEMINISM

FEMINISM is believing that all people should be treated fairly and equally, no matter their gender.

In the past, girls and women didn't have the same rights as boys and men. Girls weren't allowed to learn the same things as boys. Women weren't allowed to have the same jobs as men. Women weren't allowed to vote for the people making laws, even though the laws affected them.

Girls and women today are treated more fairly. However, there is a long way to go for equal rights for all.

FEMINISM is about making the world fairer, safer, healthier, and happier for everyone.

Learning about all kinds of people, including girls and women, helps all of us.

Read books, watch shows, and go to the movies to learn about girls and women and how they've changed the world.

See what inspires you to make the world better.

FREEDOM

FREEDOM is being able to do what you want and make your own choices. It's when you're not stopped from doing things that make you happy, healthy, and safe.

There are rules and laws that protect certain freedoms.

There are rules and laws that limit certain freedoms.

Sometimes people disagree about **FREEDOM**. They disagree about which laws they think are fair.

What kinds of freedoms are important to you?

What rules or laws help you feel safe?

What rules or laws would you like to see changed?

GOAL

A **GOAL** is something that you can work toward to accomplish.

To reach a goal, you can . . .

Practice

Play

Ask for help

Celebrate your progress

Reaching a **GOAL** can be hard work!

You might feel close to reaching your goal at one time.

Your goal might feel so far away at another time.

You might even have to start over sometimes.

Keep going! Keep telling yourself you can reach your goal. You will!

HONEST

Being **HONEST** means telling the truth and behaving in truthful ways.

There are lots of ways to be honest.

Telling the
whole truth

Admitting you did
something wrong

I broke
your toy.

Doing the
right thing

Choosing to be honest is brave.

Sometimes being **HONEST** is easy.
Sometimes being honest is hard.

When you don't tell the truth, you might hear a voice inside that lets you know you did something wrong. You might feel uncomfortable, almost like your insides are itchy. You might fidget or squirm. After you tell the truth and some time passes, you usually feel a lot better.

By being honest, you can move through the uncomfortable feelings and be proud for doing the right thing.

HOPE

HOPE is a wishful feeling. It's wanting something to happen and looking forward to it.

When you have a special event coming up, you might feel full of hope.

You might hope to have clear skies.

You might hope to catch a firefly.

You might hope to see a shooting star . . . so you can make a wish and hope it will come true!

We can **HOPE** for little things.

What is something you hope to do this week?

We can hope for big things, too.

What is something you hope for the future?

INSPIRED

When we feel **INSPIRED**, we feel excited to do or make something.

Lots of things can be sources of inspiration.

People

Art

HENRI MATISSE

Stories

Places

When we feel **INSPIRED**, we feel curious, creative, and energized.

What kinds of places
inspire you?

What kinds of people
inspire you?

What kind of art
inspires you?

What kinds of
stories inspire you?

JUSTICE

JUSTICE is about treating people in fair ways.

When there is justice, everyone is able to get what they need.

Everyone is able to live in safe homes, speak freely, breathe clean air, and drink clean water.

Everyone has the same human rights and freedoms.

Sometimes one person is treated unfairly.

Sometimes groups of people are treated unfairly.

Speaking up for **JUSTICE** is powerful.

Standing together with others makes a difference.

How can you add your unique voice to make the world more fair?

KINDNESS

KINDNESS is being thoughtful, helpful, and friendly.

It shows we care and it feels good, too.
We can . . .

Share a snack
with a friend

Help a neighbor

Send a card and flowers
to someone who is sick

What is one way you could show kindness
to someone today?

Treating ourselves with **KINDNESS** is important.

We can show ourselves love and care.

We can be kind when we talk to ourselves.

We can be kind by taking care of our bodies.

We can be kind by doing things that make us happy.

What is one way you could show kindness to yourself today?

PATIENCE

PATIENCE is the ability to stay calm while doing something for a long time.

Waiting in line for your turn takes patience.

When have you had to be patient?
What did you do to pass the time?

Sometimes we have to use **PATIENCE** when we're with other people.

We might need patience when it feels like someone is being too fast, too slow, too messy, or too loud.

We can practice being patient by thinking how others might be feeling. We can try taking a deep breath and whisper to ourselves, "I can be patient."

PEACE

We feel at **PEACE** when we feel calm, safe, and comfortable with one another.

We can add peace to our world.
When we disagree, we can . . .

Name our feelings   Listen

Have empathy   Compromise

What does peace look like to you?

Inner **PEACE** is another kind of peace, and it's just as important.

Inner peace is what happens when we are kind, patient, and loving to ourselves.

When you have inner peace, you love yourself just the way you are! You believe in yourself. You remember you are growing every day. You know you are loved.

When do you feel peaceful?

PERSEVERANCE

PERSEVERANCE is when you keep trying even when something is hard.

Learning new things takes a lot of perseverance.

Progress takes a lot of perseverance, too.

You show perseverance by doing things over and over again to reach a goal. When it gets challenging, you stick with it and don't give up.

PERSEVERANCE helps us grow, get better, and succeed.

We're able to show perseverance by saying good things and cheering ourselves on.

I can do this.

It takes time. I'll get there!

This is hard, but I can keep trying.

I'm getting better. I can stick to it.

I knew I could do it!

FINISH

REST

REST is how our brains and bodies relax and recharge.

We might rest by drawing or coloring.

We might rest by petting a dog, cat, or soft blanket.

We might rest by watching leaves rustling in the wind.

We might rest by listening to the rain, music, or even a book.

REST is important. It's a way to feed ourselves love and kindness.

Rest gives us the energy to . . .

Play

Love

Learn

Make the world better

How do you like to rest?

TEAMWORK

When we work together with other people to get something done, it's called **TEAMWORK**.

We can work as a team in our families, in our classrooms, and in our communities.

When we work as a team, we learn from others and others learn from us.

TEAMWORK is great for accomplishing big things.

As a team, we can...

Do things faster

Solve problems

Learn from one
another's mistakes

Become stronger...
together!

VOLUNTEER

To **VOLUNTEER** is to offer to help.

Some people face hard times if they're sick and trying to get better. Some people face hard times if they don't have enough food or money.

We can help make hard times easier by . . .

Raising money

Giving food

Donating toys

Cleaning up

All of us go through times when we need help, and all of us go through times when we can give help.

What are some ways you could **VOLUNTEER** your skills, your care, and your time?

We all have the power to help others in our communities and around the world.

NOTE TO ADULTS

Words matter. When children have the vocabulary to identify their own emotions, they can better understand themselves and connect with others.

When they understand and connect with others, and others understand and connect with them, they build a stronger community.

When children believe in themselves and their community, they will be inspired to make the world better for all.

This book was created to help parents, educators, and caregivers introduce words and concepts that can be challenging to explain to young children.

There's no right or wrong way to use this book. You can use these words as a starting point for new conversations with your child, or you can use them to reinforce or clarify ideas in conversations you're already having. In whatever way you use this book, we hope that your child finds a greater understanding of themselves and the world around them.

We'd also like to take this moment to acknowledge that as the world evolves, language evolves. We've done our best to provide definitions that are timely and age-appropriate. Nuances to words can change over time, and we encourage you and your child to continue reading and learning together.

For Leo and Oscar, for showing me
what matters most —J.R.D.

For my grandmother, who always
supported and inspired me —A.D.

The illustrations in this book were created in colored pencil.
Set in Annelies Pen, Quicksand, and Sofa Sans.

Cataloging-in-Publication Data has been applied for and may be
obtained from the Library of Congress.
ISBN 978-1-4197-6777-7

Text © 2023 Joanne Ruelos Diaz
Illustrations © 2023 Annelies Draws
Cover © 2023 Magic Cat
Book design by Nicola Price and Maisy Ruffels

Printed and bound in China
10 9 8 7 6 5 4 3 2 1

Abrams Books are available at special discounts when purchased in quantity for
premiums and promotions as well as fundraising or educational use. Special editions
can also be created to specification. For details, contact specialsales@abramsbooks.com
or the address below.

MIX
Paper | Supporting
responsible forestry
FSC® C109093

ABRAMS The Art of Books
195 Broadway, New York, NY 10007
abramsbooks.com